OUR SOLAR SYSTEM

The Milky Way and Other Galaxies

BY DANA MEACHEN RAU

Content Adviser: Dr. Stanley P. Jones, Assistant Director, Washington, D.C., Operations, NASA-Sponsored Classroom of the Future

Science Adviser: Terrence E. Young Jr., M.Ed., M.L.S., Jefferson Parish (Louisiana) Public School System

Reading Adviser: Susan Kesselring, M.A., Literacy Educator, Rosemount-Apple Valley-Eagan (Minnesota) School District

COMPASS POINT BOOKS

MINNEAPOLIS, MINNESOTA

For Charlie and Allison—D.M.R.

Compass Point Books
3109 West 50th Street, #115
Minneapolis, MN 55410

Visit Compass Point Books on the Internet at *www.compasspointbooks.com*
or e-mail your request to *custserv@compasspointbooks.com*

Photographs ©: Myron Jay Dorf/Corbis, cover, 1, 11; PhotoDisc, 3, 26; Roger Ressmeyer/Corbis, 4–5, 9; Mary Evans Picture Library, 6, 8 (top), 25; Bill Schoening/NOAO/AURA/NSF, 7; Bettmann/Corbis, 8 (bottom), 16; Aaron Horowitz/Corbis, 12; DigitalVision, 13 (all), 28 (bottom); Anglo-Australian Observatory, photograph by David Malin, 14; NASA Marshall Space Flight Center, 15, 20; Hillary Mathis/NOAO/AURA/NSF, 17; NOAO/AURA/NSF, 18, 21; N.A. Sharp/NOAO/AURA/NSF, 19; NASA and Hubble Heritage Team (STScI), 22–23; NASA, ESA, S. Beckwith (STScI) and the HUDF Team, 28 (top), 29.

Editor: Nadia Higgins
Lead Designer/Page production: The Design Lab
Photo researcher: Svetlana Zhurkina
Educational Consultant: Diane Smolinski

Managing Editor: Catherine Neitge
Art Director: Keith Griffin
Production Director: Keith McCormick
Creative Director: Terri Foley

Library of Congress Cataloging-in-Publication Data
Rau, Dana Meachen, 1971–
The Milky Way and other galaxies/ by Dana Meachen Rau.
    p. cm. — (Our solar system)
Includes index.
ISBN 0-7565-0853-3 (hardcover)
1. Milky Way—Juvenile literature. I. Title.
QB857.7.R38 2005
523.1'13—dc22   2004015571

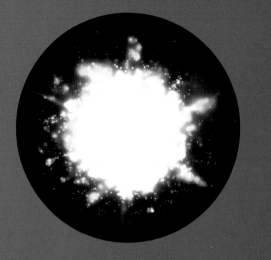

Table of Contents

A Milky Path of Stars

On clear dark nights, you can see that the sky is filled with starlight. Each twinkling point of light shows the location of a star. High over-head, you might also spot a bright, curvy path of cloudy light. It stretches across the sky from one end to the other. This cloudy path is actually made up of billions of stars. It is called the Milky Way.

We get the name *Milky Way* from the ancient Greeks. Their stories described this cloudy path of stars as a road of milk. They believed it joined their

world on Earth to the world of their gods. Other cultures in China, the Middle East, and all over the globe made up stories about the Milky Way, too. Many early sky watchers looked to the Milky Way to guide them on long journeys across open land or sea.

As huge as it seems to us, though, the Milky Way's streak of stars is just one small part of the galaxy we live in. A galaxy is a group of billions of stars as well as dust, gas, planets, and other objects in the sky that move together through space.

The word *galaxy* comes from the Greek word *gala*,

◄ *In this illustration, the Milky Way is the cloudy path of light behind Earth.*

There are 200 billion to 400 billion stars in the Milky Way Galaxy, one of which is the sun.

which means "milk." Our galaxy is called the Milky Way Galaxy after the milky-white band of light in the sky. It is also sometimes just called the Galaxy.

The Galaxy includes not only the stars in the cloudy path across the night sky, but all of the stars we can see.

Beyond these stars are more stars we can't see. The Milky Way Galaxy is just one among more than 100 billion galaxies in the universe.

The ancient Greeks made up stories ▼ about the stars they saw in the sky.

A Spinning Pinwheel

The Milky Way Galaxy is a spiral galaxy. It is shaped like a disk with a thick, bright middle. Long arms come out from the center and spiral around it. From above, our galaxy looks like a spinning pinwheel.

How do scientists know this? After all, we can't see our own galaxy—we're living in it!

Scientists have been studying the Galaxy for hundreds of years. In the 1700s, the astronomer Sir William Herschel of England

◀ *A spiral galaxy looks like a pinwheel.*

(1738–1822) looked through his telescope to try to figure out the Galaxy's shape. He counted the stars and made maps of the sky. From what he found, he believed the Galaxy was round and flat like a disk. He also believed the sun was in the center.

Many years later, in the early 1900s, Harlow Shapley (1885–1972), an American astronomer, was able to discover more details. He noticed that one part of the sky contained the most stars. He believed this area, not the

Sir William Herschel studied the Milky Way Galaxy in the 1700s. ▲

American astronomer Harlow Shapley made important observations about our galaxy. ▶

sun, was the thick, bright center of the Galaxy. He also believed the band of light across the sky was actually our view of one of the arms coming out from the center.

Scientists have also been studying other galaxies for clues of how our galaxy is shaped. The nearby Andromeda Galaxy, which is spiral-shaped much like our own, has provided valuable information for scientists.

◀ *The center of the Milky Way Galaxy is crowded with stars.*

Andromeda is the farthest galaxy from Earth that can be seen without a telescope.

The sun, Earth, and all the other planets in our solar system are located on one of the Galaxy's arms. Our solar system is toward the outer edge of the Galaxy. It is about two-thirds of the distance from the center to the edge of the disk.

The Milky Way Galaxy is so huge that it is hard to imagine its size. Space objects as large as a galaxy are measured in light-years. When you flip on a light switch, it seems as if the light of a lamp instantly appears. The light has actually traveled from the lamp to your eyes. Light moves faster than anything else in the universe. A light-year is the distance that light travels in one year at a rate of 186,282 miles per second (298,051 kilometers per second). That distance is nearly 6 trillion miles (9.6 trillion km), which is considered one light-year. Our galaxy is 100,000 light-years from edge to edge. The sun and our solar system are about 30,000 light-years from the center of the Galaxy.

Our solar system is constantly moving within the Galaxy, though it always stays the same distance away from the center. Our solar system travels around the center of the Galaxy in a path called an orbit. Its journey all the way around takes quite a while. One trip takes 250 million years. This is called the sun's cosmic year.

Our solar system orbits the center of the Galaxy on one of its arms. ▼

100,000 light-years

30,000 light-years

Earth and our solar system

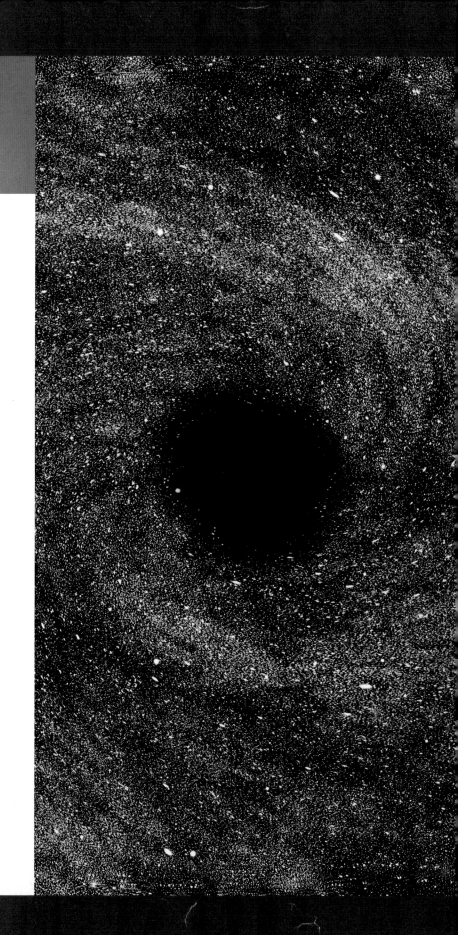

Parts of the Milky Way

★.★ The Milky Way Galaxy has three main parts.

The center of the Galaxy, called the bulge, is the brightest area. That is because it is crowded with many stars. The stars in the bulge are about 10 billion years old. Scientists believe the bulge might contain a black hole. A black hole is an area of space with incredibly strong gravity. Gravity is a force that pulls objects toward a center. The billions of stars of the Milky Way

Black holes, such as the one in this ▶ illustration, may hold galaxies together.

arm
(side view)

bulge

halo

are held together by this strong gravity.

The Galaxy's arms are where you find our sun and the rest of the solar system. You also find many other stars and clouds of gas and dust. The arms are the area of the Galaxy where new stars are born. This happens when these gassy dust clouds come together. The other stars in the arms, such as our sun, are young, too. The sun is about 5 billion years old. That doesn't seem very young, but compared to the rest of the Galaxy it is.

▲ *Gassy dust clouds called nebulae are found in the Galaxy's arms.*

◄ *A side view a galaxy similar to the Milky Way, showing its three main parts*

A halo surrounds the disk. It is a ball-shaped area containing groups of some of the oldest stars in the universe—about 15 billion years old. That is when scientists believe the universe began. Studying these stars is like looking back in time to what the universe was like when it was forming.

Groups of stars in the Galaxy's halo, called globular clusters, contain some of the oldest stars in the universe.

Big clouds of dust block large parts of the Milky Way from view. To study these areas, scientists use radio or X-ray telescopes, such as the Chandra X-ray Observatory pictured here. These special telescopes measure the energy from stars.

Types of Galaxies

In the 1920s, an American astronomer named Edwin Hubble (1889–1953) spent much of his time looking through a telescope at the Mount Wilson Observatory in Pasadena, California. He was trying to learn as much as he could about galaxies. He discovered that there are many more galaxies than just the Milky Way—billions, in fact. And each galaxy has millions or billions of stars.

American astronomer Edwin Hubble ▶
studied galaxies in the 1920s.

Galaxies can be grouped into a few types. Spiral galaxies, such as the Milky Way, have bright centers surrounded by flat disks of young stars, gas, and dust. A barred spiral galaxy has a "bar" of stars across its center. Like a regular spiral galaxy, it has arms. However, they seem to come out of the bar instead of the center. Some scientists believe that the Milky Way may be a barred spiral.

Most galaxies in the universe are elliptical galaxies.

An elliptical galaxy

They look like fat, fuzzy eggs or footballs, and they do not have arms. They vary greatly in size. Some of the very largest and some of the smallest galaxies in the universe are elliptical. They are filled with stars and barely any gas or dust. Since stars are formed from dust clouds, few new stars are created in an elliptical galaxy. Almost all the stars in it are very old.

Irregular galaxies are neither spiral nor elliptical. They do not have a definite shape. They often look like clouds and orbit other galaxies.

Another type of galaxy is named for how it acts, not for how it is shaped. Active

An irregular galaxy

galaxies give off far more energy than other galaxies. These galaxies are much brighter than most other galaxies, too, even though they are very far away from us.

Active galaxies give off incredible amounts of energy. ▶

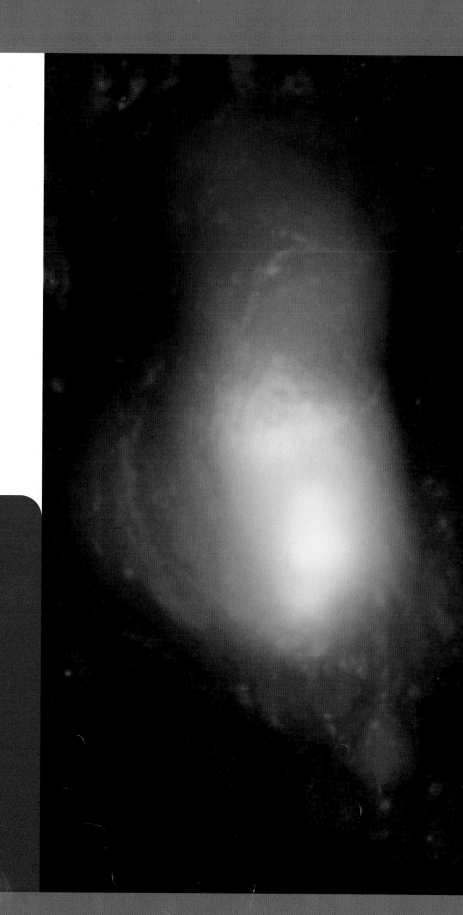

A quasar is an object at the center of some active galaxies. Most quasars are about the size of our solar system. A single quasar can give off 1,000 times as much energy as the whole Milky Way Galaxy and is a trillion times brighter than the sun.

Groups of Galaxies

The stars of the Milky Way are held together by gravity. Gravity also holds groups of galaxies together in clusters. Our galaxy is part of a cluster called the Local Group.

There are 30 to 40 galaxies in the Local Group. Of these, the Milky Way Galaxy is the second largest. It is one of only three spiral galaxies in the group. The rest of the galaxies are elliptical or irregular. Most are very

◀ *A cluster of galaxies*

small elliptical galaxies called dwarf galaxies.

Two irregular galaxies orbit the Milky Way. The Large Magellanic Cloud and the Small Magellanic Cloud look like blurry splotches in the night sky.

Gravity is always pulling the galaxies in the Local Group toward one another. In fact, the Andromeda Galaxy is moving toward the Milky Way at a speed of 62 miles (99 km) a second! That means someday Andromeda and the Milky Way may

Two spiral galaxies pass by each other. ▶

join together as one large galaxy.

The Milky Way is also always pulling on the Magellanic Clouds. Stars may even move from one galaxy to another.

There are many other galaxy clusters in the universe besides our Local Group. Our cluster is rather small. Some clusters may have thousands of galaxies.

Clusters are also grouped together into even larger groups called superclusters. Our Local Group is part of a supercluster that contains about 400 other clusters of galaxies.

The universe is filled with many superclusters. It makes our massive Milky Way seem rather small in comparison!

Ferdinand Magellan ▶

The Large Magellanic Cloud and the Small Magellanic Cloud are named after Ferdinand Magellan (1480?–1521), an explorer from the 1500s. The galaxies guided him as he sailed the seas of the southern parts of Earth.

Always on the Move

When Hubble studied galaxies in the 1920s, he noticed that they all seemed to be moving through space. For the most part, the areas between the galaxies grew bigger over time. Hubble discovered that the universe was expanding. Today, this idea is called Hubble's Law.

If you could reverse time, the galaxies of the universe would be rushing closer to each other instead of spreading out. Scientists believe that about 15 billion years ago,

Scientists think the universe began with ▸ a huge explosion called the Big Bang.

everything that makes up the universe was packed into a tiny point. This point was so small you would not even be able to see it without a microscope. Because so much material was squeezed into a tiny space, the point was incredibly hot. Eventually, it exploded. This explosion, which marks the beginning of the universe, is called the Big Bang.

Everything flew out into space. Then it started to cool. After millions of years, gas formed. Then clouds formed. Even though the universe was growing, gravity started pulling some of the gassy clouds together.

Scientists disagree about what exactly happened next. According to one idea, some clouds of gases began spinning to form thick centers and thin disks. Stars formed in the clouds. These became galaxies. This may be how the Milky Way and other galaxies formed about 10 billion years ago.

The force of the Big Bang is still causing galaxies to fly through space. Our Local Group travels at about 350 miles (560 km) per second. That's a fast ride! Will we fly through space like this forever? Will we ever slow down?

Some scientists think the universe may keep expanding. They

believe in an open universe. Others think the galaxies may slow down. Gravity will pull them back together, and they will condense down again to a single point. They believe in a closed universe.

Whatever does happen, it is billions and billions of years away. For now, we can enjoy the view from Earth. As you gaze up into the night sky, think about the Milky Way Galaxy. It is on a journey, traveling with other galaxies through the vast and unknown universe.

The Hubble Space Telescope, named after the astronomer Edwin Hubble, orbits Earth. It takes photos of distant galaxies such as the one above. ▶

Milky Way Facts

Milky Way Galaxy:
- 100,000 light-years across
- bulge: 10,000 light-years thick
- disk: 1,000 light-years thick
- Contains 200 billion to 400 billion stars
- 10 billion years old

Sun:
- 30,000 light-years from the center of the Galaxy
- Travels 155 miles (248 km) per second around the center of the Galaxy
- Takes 200 million to 250 million years to orbit the Galaxy once
- 5 billion years old

Local Group:
- 5 million light-years across
- Contains 30 to 40 galaxies

Glossary

Big Bang—the enormous explosion that created the universe about 15 billion years ago, according to one widely believed scientific theory

black hole—an area of space with such incredibly strong gravity that nothing—including light—can get out of it; scientists believe huge black holes are at the centers of most galaxies

bulge—the center of a spiral galaxy

elliptical—oval-shaped

gravity—the force that pulls objects to its center; Earth's gravity causes objects to drop to the ground

Hubble's Law—the observation, made by Edwin Hubble, that galaxies are moving away from each other and that the galaxies farthest away from ours are moving the fastest

telescope—a tool used by astronomers to collect information about distant objects; many important telescopes are not on Earth, but in outer space

X-ray—a strong, invisible beam of energy that can be detected by special telescopes

Did You Know?

- The Milky Way's path across the sky is not always clear. There are dark spots of dusty clouds. One very dark part is called the Great Rift.

- In the 1600s, Galileo Galilei (1564–1642), an Italian astronomer, was the first to realize that the milky band of light across the sky was actually made up of billions of stars.

- Scientists sometimes call superclusters "galactic zoos" because they contain almost every type of galaxy—just as a zoo has every type of animal.

- The Maiden's Festival is celebrated in China. It is based on a story about a princess and her shepherd husband. The two are separated by a silver stream—the Milky Way. One day of the year they are allowed to cross the stream to be together.

- Besides Andromeda, only two other galaxies can be seen without a telescope. These two galaxies are the Large Magellanic Cloud and the Small Magellanic Cloud. Andromeda can only be seen in the northern part of Earth, and the Magellanic Clouds can only be seen in the south.

Want to Know More?

AT THE LIBRARY

Ford, Harry. *The Young Astronomer*. New York: Dorling Kindersley, 1998.

Gifford, Clive. *The Kingfisher Facts and Records Book of Space*. New York: Kingfisher, 2001.

Mitton, Jacqueline, and Simon Mitton. *Scholastic Encyclopedia of Space*. New York: Scholastic, 1999.

Vogt, Gregory L. *Deep Space Astronomy*. Brookfield, Conn.: Twenty-First Century Books, 1999.

ON THE WEB

For more information on the **Milky Way,** use FactHound to track down Web sites related to this book.

1. Go to *www.facthound.com*
2. Type in a search word related to this book or this book ID: **0756508533**.
3. Click on the *Fetch It* button.

Your trusty FactHound will fetch the best Web sites for you!

ON THE ROAD

Adler Planetarium and Astronomy Museum

1300 S. Lake Shore Drive

Chicago, IL 60605-2403

312/922-STAR

To visit the oldest planetarium in the Western Hemisphere

National Air and Space Museum

Sixth and Independence Avenue Southwest

Washington, DC 20560

202/357-2700

To learn more about the solar system and space exploration

National Radio Astronomy Observatory

The Very Large Array

P.O. Box O

1003 Lopezville Road

Socorro, NM 87801-0387

505/835-7000

To see a collection of 27 radio antennae that are always collecting the energy coming from deep space

Mount Wilson Observatory

Mount Wilson, CA 91023

626/793-3100

To see the telescope that many famous astronomers have used to study the night sky

Index

◄ **About the Author:** *Dana Meachen Rau loves to study space. Her office walls are covered with pictures of planets, astronauts, and spacecraft. She also likes to look up at the sky with her telescope and write poems about what she sees. Ms. Rau is the author of more than 100 books for children, including nonfiction, biographies, storybooks, and early readers. She lives in Burlington, Connecticut, with her husband, Chris, and children, Charlie and Allison.*